Denmark

Den

mark

GRØNLUND'S FORLAG

The landscape of East Jutland, compared to conditions in other regions of Denmark, was formed rather dramatically - moulded by melt water from the ice cap. Water collected under the ice into rivers which cut deep elongated valleys in the ground. Vejle Ådal is one of these melt water valleys.

Roskilde Fjord on Zealand was crowded with ships in Viking times; both warships and trading vessels. Today, sailing in Viking ships can be experienced in exact replicas. In the background can be seen Roskilde Cathedral, the oldest part of which is from the 13th century. The cathedral is the burial place of the Danish kings. The first royal interment took place in 1413. The deceased monarch was Queen Margrete I - see the following pages.

Ice formed the land

Denmark was formed by ice over a period of a million years. Large areas of North Europe were covered by an ice cap - just as most of Greenland is today.

The last time the ice cap receded was about 15-20,000 years ago which caused the land masses to buckle when freed from the pressure of the ice. After they had more or less settled again - in geological terms the land is not yet entirely stable - the land bridge which linked Central Europe with the Scandinavian peninsular had become an island realm.

old, but these hunters were forced back by the ice cap, which following an almost ice free period, again moved from north to south.

Today the Danish landscape is marked everywhere by people and their activities. Over most of Denmark, the landscape is dotted with buildings as far as the eye can see: Hamlets, village settlements, churches, larger towns - and a city measurable by modern European standards. This is Copenhagen, which is the administrative centre even though the city is by no means the

Subsequently, this island realm has changed in appearance several times. The sea level has risen and fallen and reformed the land. Wind and sea have smoothed out the contours of the landscape; but the land and landscape have retained the main features created by the melting ice.

It is supposed that Denmark's land mass became ice free just under 12,000 years ago, which coincided with the first influx of permanent settlers. Actually, there are traces of human activity (hunting of larger animals) which can be accurately dated to be about 50,000 years

present geographical centre of the country. Copenhagen also accommodates the royal residence.

The first attempt to establish a national unitary state is difficult to place historically. "Historical times" starts in Denmark about 1,000 years ago - with the kings at the time of the Vikings.

Since then, Denmark has had monarchs in an unbroken line, which is unique in the world. There have been 50 kings and two reigning queens.

The little blue-eyed princess

"And could I do it so that people need not be ashamed of me?"

These words were spoken on 15th January 1972 from a balcony at Christiansborg in Copenhagen by a 31 year old woman dressed in mourning and with tears in her eyes. The previous day she had lost her father to whom she was very close and loved dearly. Her father was Frederik IX (1899-1972).

Before the young queen spoke, Denmark's Prime Minister, in accordance with Danish democratic custom, had called out towards three corners of the world "King Frederik IX is dead! Long live Her Majesty Queen Margrethe II!"

A quarter of a century after that cold January day in 1972, public opinion polls have several times sought to pinpoint the people's attitude to the constitutional monarchy.
Over 90% of the population approves of Margrethe II. Even deep in the ranks of socialist and republican circles, the Queen is liked and admired.

Margrethe II and Prince Henrik in the royal palace, Amalienborg, in Copenhagen. The Prince is wearing the dress uniform of the Royal Lifeguards, and both the Queen and Prince bear Denmark's oldest and most distinguished decoration: The order of the Elephant. It was founded in the 1470s by Christian I. The white-enamelled gold elephant may either be suspended on a chain consisting of small gold elephants, or - as here - on a blue ribbon worn over the left shoulder.

Should the almost unthinkable happen, that Denmark had to give up the monarchy and become a republic, Margrethe II would undoubtedly become Denmark's first democratically elected president.

Margrethe Alexandrine Thorhildur Ingrid was born on 16th April 1940, the eldest daughter of the then Crown Prince Frederik and Princess Ingrid (born in Sweden in 1910). A few days before - 9th April - a hugely superior air, land and naval force from Nazi Germany had attacked and occupied an almost defenceless Denmark.
The mood in Denmark for the vast majority was black despair. The birth of a princess was a national event - a hope for the future.

The medical team who had assisted at the rather difficult birth spoke of "the lovely, tiny, blue-eyed princess" - even though they well knew that all newborn babies have blue eyes and are quite small. Princess Margrethe weighed 3,300 grams at birth.

On 10th June 1967 in Copenhagen, Crown Princess Margrethe was married to the French diplomat Henri-Marie-Jean-André, Count de Laborde de Monpezat. With peace in Europe and the widespread use of television, the wedding of the Heir to the Throne and Prince Henrik was not only a national, but also an international event.

The Crown Princess and the diplomat had met each other in London, and their meeting, as expressed by the later Queen Margrethe II, was "Love at first sight, so that the sky exploded."

Like his wife, the Prince Consort is well-read, intellectual and artistically talented. Amongst other things he is an excellent pianist. Together with Queen Margrethe, he has translated the French author Simone de Beauvoir's philosophical novel "All Men Are Mortal". Queen Margrethe's literary translations embrace a number of titles, including Eric Linklater's "The Wind on the Moon". The Queen's artistic endeavours cover scenography work for theatre and television, including the costumes for a much praised ballet version of Hans Christian Andersen's "The Shepherdess and the Chimney Sweep". Collaborating with the British author J.R.R. Tolkien, the Queen has illustrated an edition of his "Lord of the Rings". The Queen has also created small works of art such as the postage stamp "5th May 1945-85". The date 5.5.1945 is the official date of Denmark's liberation after the German capitulation the evening before.

Margrethe II is a hyper-active lady. So was her predecessor and namesake in the long line of Danish monarchs, but in a different way. Margrete I (1353-1412) was not a reigning monarch according to constitutional conceptions both then and nowadays. Nevertheless, there has never been an official ruler in Scandinavia who has reigned so purposefully, effectively and successfully as she. She reigned as regent; first for her son Oluf, and later for her princely foster son Erik, who, as a six year old, was subjected to her undoubtedly masterful upbringing.

Through family politics and a policy of fusing estates, Margrete I created a royal fellowship between Denmark, Norway (with Iceland) and Sweden (with Finland). In 1397, her foster son Erik was crowned king of all three kingdoms. The union was maintained until 1523, when Sweden broke away.

Since the dissolution of the union, there have been a number of bloody wars between the three Scandinavian countries. Today things are very peaceful.
For example, Queen Margrethe and Norway's Queen Sonja spend a week together every year - skiing in Norway or Greenland, living in primitive cabins and doing their own cooking.

The Queen and Prince Henrik have renovated a small chateau near Cahors in France. This is where Prince Henrik produces his own wine and here he and the Queen spend their Summer holidays.

7

The next generation in the Royal Family

"Of course, one watches how one's mother has done it, but I have had a different upbringing, and I live in a different time".

The words are those of Margrethe II and Prince Henrik's eldest son who was born on 26th May 1968. Unless something unexpected happens, some time in this century, Frederik André Henrik Christian, Prince of Denmark, will become Frederik X of Denmark - as the sixth member of the royal house of Glücksborg and the 53rd head of state in the world's oldest monarchy.

Crown Prince Frederik is undoubtedly the best prepared heir to the Danish throne of all time.
Military training and a reasonable insight into academic thought has always been a tradition in the Danish Royal Family. Crown Prince Frederik has insisted on taking military training to the utmost limits with free-fall parachute jumping and scuba diving to great depths.
He also insisted on completing a standard university course ending with an academic degree in political science (Århus University, Harvard University).

The Heir to the Throne was not content with the usual courtesy visit to the United Nations headquarters in New York.
He insisted on performing a proper job for three months in the Danish United Nations Mission and wrote his own speech for the General Assembly.

As a young man, Crown Prince Frederik has never lacked female company. However, (as far as we know) he has not yet chosen a wife. According to the Danish law of succession, a condition for succession to the throne is that the heir apparent's marriage is approved by both the Queen and the government.

The same condition applies to number two in the Danish succession, the Crown Prince's younger brother, Prince Joachim (born 1969).
He has presented his sweetheart as a marriage partner, and their mutual choice has been approved by the Queen and the government.
And not least by the people, who were taken by surprise on the announcement of the engagement.
Royal marriage partners from surrounding countries have been the rule throughout the Danish monarchy's more than a thousand year history; but a Danish princess from the other end of the world...!

Crown Prince Frederik of Denmark has a more extensive education, both civil and military than any other heir apparent before him.

The little dark-haired beauty (Princess Alexandra is 1.62 m tall) was received in Denmark with great curiosity, but also much warmth and kindness. After a short period meeting many people in Denmark, one can say with justification and using an old Danish idiom, that her charm and charisma "took the Danes by storm".

Alexandra Christina Manley - after her marriage to Prince Joachim, Princess Alexandra of Denmark - was born in the former British Crown Colony of Hongkong in 1964, which according to the Chinese calendar, is the Year of the Dragon.

Both Princess Alexandra and Prince Joachim have a business training.
Besides which, Prince Joachim has a solid education in agriculture. The pair own and run the Schackenborg estate at Møgeltønder in South Jutland.

In the extensive and exhaustive descriptions of the engagement and royal wedding, it was sometimes pointed out that Princess Alexandra has the same name as another Danish princess. She was the daughter of Christian IX (1818-1906), and as was the case with several other of his daughters, was married to an heir apparent, namely the Prince of Wales, later Edward VII of Great Britain (1841-1910). This queen of England is still known by the nickname "The Beloved Lady".

Princess Alexandra and Prince Joachim in the royal reception rooms in Christiansborg castle in Copenhagen. The picture was taken on the evening before their wedding, and Princess Alexandra had just been made an official member of the Danish royal family. On a blue ribbon worn over her left shoulder, the Princess bears the white-enamelled gold elephant.

Union in the North Atlantic

Air travellers flying over Greenland - the world's largest island - obtain a dramatic impression of what Northern Europe with Denmark looked like 15-20,000 years ago.

The enormous expanse of inland ice has an incredibly rugged surface. Especially near the edges, the ice is split by deep ravines, up to 20m wide and 50 m deep. Naked mountain peaks rear up over the ice, and from the many glaciers, the ice slides out into the sea as icebergs; many of them are huge in size and have strange shapes.

The enormous island has an overall area of 2,175,600 sq.km (840,000 sq.miles). Out of this, 1,833,900 sq.km (775,221 sq.m) are covered by the 2 km (1.25 miles) thick ice cap. The ice free areas around the coast are settled. The Greenlandic name for the country is Kalaallit Nunaat i.e. The Peoples' Land.

Greenlanders are the descendants of Eskimo tribes that migrated about 1300 A.D. and since then have mingled with Europeans; e.g. whalers and Danish colonists. The

In geological terms, Greenland is part of the North American continent, but separated from the northernmost part of America and therefore a "genuine" island.
Greenland has an arctic climate, but nevertheless a rich flora and fauna. Among the most impressive of the larger mammals can be found the polar bear, musk ox and walrus.

The rocky landscape of the Faroes is rugged, but fertile.

population is about 50,000 of which 6,000 are from Denmark. (Personnel from Danish and American military camps are not included).

For centuries, Greenland's main occupation was hunting, especially for seals. The hunters' catch made Greenland self-sufficient; not only with meat, but also with fuel and lamp oil (from blubber), clothes, tents and boats (from hides). Hunting is still an important industry, but on the whole, it is not enough in modern Greenland. The new main industry is fishing. There has also been mining in several places in Greenland; for coal, cryolite, zinc and lead. At the moment there is only one coal mine in operation, but various companies are at present prospecting for both hard minerals and oil.

Greenland has been "an autonomous community within the Danish kingdom" since 1979 - the same as the Faroe Islands, the other area in the North Atlantic which has a national union with Denmark. The self-governing principle applies in both cases; i.e. that legislation and administration occurs locally within the framework laid down for the kingdom. Some areas, such as foreign policy, the state church and the police are common policy affairs which are controlled by the central authority. Greenland and the Faroes each send two members to the Danish Parliament "Folketinget".

The Faroes have had self-government within the Danish kingdom since 1948. The rocky islands in the North Atlantic with their grass-covered mountain sides are known as "The Green Islands".

The Faroe Islands, which consist of volcanic mountain rock, are the remnants of a much larger area. Geological forces have eroded most of this territory and left the Faroes as islands separated by narrow straits.
Today there are 17 inhabited and a dozen uninhabited islands.

The climate is mild, though with much wind and rain. Apart from grass, the vegetation is sparse.
There are only a few, small species of wild animals, but the cliffs and mountain sides are rich in bird-life.

The total area of the Faroes is 1,399 sq.km (540 sq.miles). The largest of the islands, Streymøy or "Stream Island" has an area of 374 sq.km (144 sq.m.).

The Faroes were inhabited by migrating Norwegians in the 10th century, i.e. in the time of the Vikings. Their descendants, some of whom possibly have Celtic blood in their veins, today make up a Faroese population of about 40,000. The main industry is fishing. There is extensive sheep farming and bird trapping on the mountain sides.
A third large inhabited area in the North Atlantic was also formerly a part of the Danish Union. This is Iceland, which voted to become an independent republic in 1941.

The historical background for the union between

Denmark, the Faroes and Greenland is the centuries old United Kingdom of Denmark and Norway which was dissolved in 1814. Over the centuries, these "twin kingdoms" together built up their own little world-wide "empire". At its peak, apart from the North Atlantic territories, it consisted of colonies in India (Tranquebar and the Nicobar Islands in the Indian Ocean), the Virgin Islands in the Caribbean (now under the U.S.A.) and a territory in West Africa.

Time and again, usually when the kingdom's joint economy is under discussion in political assemblies, one hear the question:

"What do we want with The Faroes and Greenland?"

In Denmark, there is a large majority in favour of keeping the union intact - one reason probably being the many personal contacts between Danes, Faroe Islanders and Greenlanders. Therefore the almost classic reply to the question is: "We should be pleased to have them."

Facts about Denmark

Unless the after effects of the last glacial period together with the wind and the sea drastically change its shape and area, and not counting the autonomous areas Greenland and the Faroes, Denmark actually consists of the peninsular of Jutland and about 480 islands, 90 of which are inhabited (1997).

The total land area changes slightly the whole time. It is about 43,000 sq.km (17,000 sq.miles). Jutland's area is calculated to be about 29,600 sq.km (11,500 sq.m) and the largest islands as follows:

Zealand: 7,015 sq.km (2,709 sq.m.)
Funen: 2,984 sq.km.(1.152 sq.m.)
Lolland: 1,234 sq.km (480 sq.m.)
Bornholm: 588 sq.km (227 sq.m.)

Denmark has only one land frontier - the boundary between Denmark and the Federal Republic of Germany. This has changed from time to time, but nowadays always by agreement between Danish and German neighbours wanting to change the shape and extent of their territories. The length of the border is only about 67.7 km (40 miles).

Denmark's total coastline is 7,300 km (4,563 miles).

Denmark has a temperate coastal climate. The hottest month is July, the coldest, January. Cloud cover is least in May and greatest in December. May and June give the most sunshine, December the least. The lowest temperature measured in Denmark is -31°C, the highest measured is 36°C.
Denmark's population is between 5.1 and 5.2 million, of which one third lives in the vicinity of the capital city. That is the densely populated city area of Copenhagen plus the three adjacent counties.
The legislative assembly, Folketinget, is a single chamber parliament, elected for a four-year period by ordinary direct vote. The parliament has 179 members, of whom 4 are elected by the autonomous communities in the North Atlantic: two from the Faroes and two from Greenland.

The Prime Minister has the power to declare an election prematurely, before the elapse of the four year period.

Denmark is a member of the European Community, United Nations, NATO and the Nordic Council. The Danish church is evangelical-Lutheran.

Currency: Danish crown (DKK), 1 crown = 100 øre.

In order to understand the names of Danish places shown in the photos, it is practical to know the meaning of a few of the words which occur most frequently.

Kirke = church
gård = farm (often used as a suffix)
havn = harbour
borg = fortress (usually a suffix). Originally it meant a fortified castle and has subsequently been used in names of towns that have grown up around a fort.

At the tip of Denmark

For hundreds of years in North Jutland, there has in many instances been a sharp distinction between "north of the fjord" and "south of the fjord".

The fjord is *Limfjord,* which strictly speaking is not a fjord, but a strait. Limfjord connects Kattegat with the North Sea and divides what geologists and geographers

in those south of the fjord. Naturally, the reverse is also the case.

Limfjord is 180 km (70 miles) long. Its form is extremely irregular, alternating between narrow straits and extensive broads. The largest island in Limfjord is Mors, which is considered to be an "independent" area north of the fjord. The other North Jutland areas are Thy, Hansherred, and by far the largest, Vendsyssel.

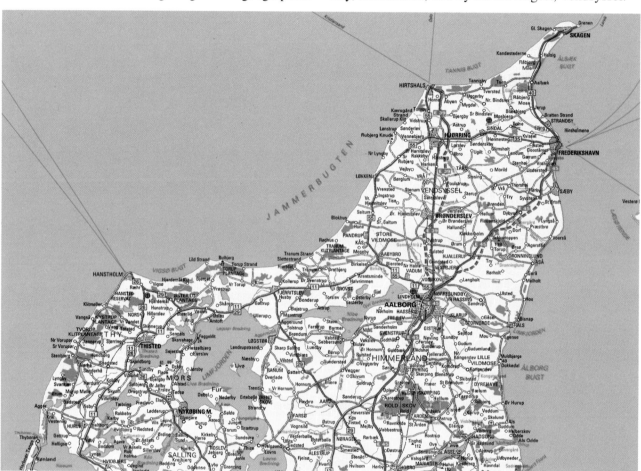

call the "North Jutland Island" from the rest of Jutland. All the landlinks which cross Limfjord today are man-made.

Today, the area north of Limfjord is considered to be a part of Jutland, and not an island. However, there is still a schism between north and south of the fjord. This occurs in a good-natured form of teasing, where in the native inhabitants north of the fjord are convinced that they possess qualities completely lacking

Until the beginning of last century, when the first bridge over Limfjorden was opened, the areas north of the fjord were rather isolated from the rest of Denmark. One could sail across, but that was only for the relatively few.

Traces of these many hundreds of years of isolation are apparent today - most prominently maybe in language. The original Vendsyssel dialect - which is still spoken by many of the "natives" - bears very little resemblance to any of the other dialects in Denmark, of which there are many. By linguistic standards, it is not really a dialect, but rather an original language: It is significantly similar to Scottish, in vocabulary, grammar and syntax.

The historical explanation for this phenomenon is to be found in the Viking Age. Those Vikings who set sail from the northernmost part of the west coast of Jutland with Great Britain as their course, landed in Scotland; while their warrior counterparts who embarked further down the west coast of Jutland, landed in England.

As it was the Vikings' custom to take beautiful maidens home with them, the Scottish girls were landed in Vendsyssel after a raid. They became the progenitors of generation after generation of mothers who raised their children with a language which was just as much Scottish as Danish.

A song of praise to Jutland written by the storyteller Hans Christian Andersen is called "Jutland Between Two Seas". These are Kattegat and Skagerrak that meet at the northenmost tip of Denmark, *The Cape of Skaw.*

The Cape of Skaw with the town *Skagen* about 2 km from the north tip is a world famous place. This is mostly because of the meeting of the two seas - and the reflection of sunlight on the surface of the ocean towards both east and west. It is termed "The light over Skaw" in artistic circles. During the 1870s, a group of prominent painters worked at Skaw. The most famous members of this artists' colony are *Michael Ancher and P.S. Krøyer.*

Today, one can ride over the Cape of Skaw in a small tractor-drawn train called *"Sandormen"* (The Lugworm). *Lighthouses* from different periods can also be seen on the spit of land. The oldest known type of lighthouse has a brazier as the source of light. This type is called a *"bascule light"*.

Just as lighthouses remind one of the dangers of the

sea, so is *"Den tilsandede Kirke"* (The sand covered church) reminiscent of the ravages caused by wind and shifting sands. The old church at the Skaw was demolished in 1795 - except for the tower which served as a landmark for seafarers.

In time, it was dicovered that the movement of the sand could be limited by planting the dunes. An unplanted "wandering dune" can still be found though; *Råbjerg Mile* - and a dramatic example of the ravages caused by shifting sand and the sea's erosion of the coast can be seen at *Rubjerg Knude.*

North Jutland's largest city - and Denmark's fourth largest - is *Aalborg* on the south side of Limfjord. It is a very lively city in spite of its age - the oldest known trace of the town is from about 1000 A.D. *The cathedral, St. Budolfi* was built about 1440 and named after a saint who was the patron of seafarers. *Jens Bangs Stenhus* from 1624 (Jens Bangs Stonehouse) is undoubtedly the best-preserved Renaissance building in the whole of Scandinavia.

25 km south of Aalborg lies Rebild Bakker, the Danish-American national park, which is the venue each year on the 4th July, the USA's Independence Day, for a traditional celebration. In 1962, about 50,000 people gathered in the park to celebrate its 50 years jubilee; many of them were descendants of Danish emigrants to the United States.

As in every other part of the country, North Jutland contains both ecclesiastical and secular architecture which is well worth examining.

Spøttrup is one of Denmark's best-preserved fortresses from the late middle ages, built about 1500 A.D.

Voergård is famous for its east wing with corner towers, and a lavishly decorated sandstone portal inspired by ancient triumphal arches.

"Sandormen"

Vippefyret

Skagen

Skagen Fyr

Grenen

Grenen

Grenen

Skagen Havn

DANSK FISKER OG REDNINGSMAND

Skagen Museum

The harsh weather has influenced the architecture. As neighbour to the North Sea, it's not only for looks that the red roofs are strengthened with white-washed pointing.

Gl. Skagen (Højen)

Skagen

Rubjerg Knude

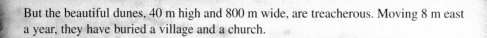

But the beautiful dunes, 40 m high and 800 m wide, are treacherous. Moving 8 m east a year, they have buried a village and a church.

RÅBJERG MILE is its name, and beautiful it is. So is the surrounding countryside. And precisely because the climate is so harsh, one marvels at the richness of the flora. Bilberries and cotton grass, heather and wild orchids, and the rare, insect-eating sundew hide in sheltered hollows.

Rubjerg Knude

Krudttårnet, Frederikshavn

At **Frederikshavn** on Jutland's east coast, sheltered from the stiff, prevaling winds, the land changes character. The beaches are not spectacular perhaps but better for children, and the country-side is more fertile. In the midst of the large, bustling harbour - with its many ferry connections to Norway and Sweden - is the Krudttårn Museum.

Voer Kirke, Flauenskjold

Beautiful sandy beaches stretch from Skagen and 400 km south, one of the most splendid landscapes in Denmark. In many places you can drive your car down on the beach and a five-minute walk will take you to your own private paradise among the high sand dunes. In summer, the beaches are dominated by holiday-makers enjoying being in or on the water. In winter, these same beaches are the harsh workplace of fishermen who still pull their boats up onto the beach in many places for want of a harbour.

Løkken

Sankt Budolfi Kirke

Jens Bangs Stenhus

AALBORG. The Cathedral and Merchant Jens Bang's Stone House bear witness of the town's significance in the Middle Ages and Renaissance. Its importance today is shown by its university centre, industries, shipping, "legendary" night life, and not least its cultural life.

Jomfru Ane Gade

Lindholm Høje

High above the Limfjord is **Lindholm Høje,** the largest Viking burial place in the North. The many objects found during excavation of the 682 graves can be seen in the Aalborg History Museum.

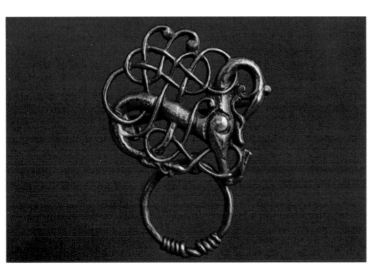

Klitmøller

Spøttrup Castle from about 1400, with its double moat, remains as it was in the Middle Ages.

Voergård, built in 1590 by Ingeborg Skeel, with its fine collection of furniture and art is one of our best preserved Renaissance castles.

Central Jutland

A land of contrasts

Nearly all the different forms of landscape that were created by the ice cap can be observed in Mid-Jutland: in the east, fjords and a landscape with deep valleys, while further in, rolling hills with lakes and streams; in the west, flat plains changing to sand dune formations on the west coast.

During the latest geological period on earth, the Quarternary period, there were six ice ages in Northern Europe and five warmer periods in between when the

sq.km (386 sq.miles) and there are only two towns of any size, Skanderborg in the east and Silkeborg to the north.

Himmelbjerget (Sky Mountain) south of Julsø appears to be the highest point in this highland lake terrain, because the hill rises so steeply from a lake. In reality, there are two even higher peaks in the landscape: Ejer Bavnehøj, and Yding Skovhøj which is the highest "mountain" in the country - all of 173 m high!
Himmelbjerget attracts by far the most visitors to the district.

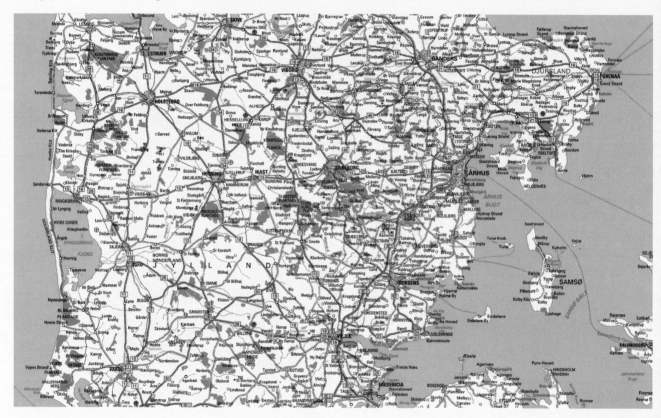

ice receded. During five of these glacial periods, the whole of Denmark was covered by the ice cap. During the sixth glacial period there were ice free areas in Jutland. The undulating landscape was formed beneath the ice cover and during the retreat of the ice: the flat areas were created by melt water streaming from the ice masses.

A large, coherent area of land in Central Jutland appears, by Danish standards, to be "untouched nature". The area is named "Det midtjyske Søhøjland" (The mid Jutland Lake District). It encompasses 1,000

The many water courses in the area - first and foremost the Gudenå river system - have supplied energy for centuries, principally for grinding corn in water mills. The first industry in the district also used water power from Gudenå. This was Silkeborg Paper Factory which was opened in 1845.

The paddle steamer *"Hjejlen"* has been a tourist attraction on the lakes for more than a hundred years.
In Central Jutland, there are remnants of the earliest vegetation after the last glacial period. These are in the areas of heathland, which in technical language are

called "lynghede" (heather moorland) or "dværg-buskhede" (scrub moorland). Most of the original extensive heathlands in Jutland are today either cultivated or planted with fir trees. Those areas, which remain untouched, are now mostly protected areas. One of them is *Hjerl Hede* east of Vinderup. Here can be found "Hjerl Hedes Frilandsmuseum", an open-air museum containing amongst others, Denmark's oldest farm building "Vinkelgården" and the reconstruction of a stone age settlement; i.e. the period after the last ice age when migrants first settled.

Central Jutland is rich in manor house culture. *Gammel Estrup,* which has medieval origins but today is characterised by its reconstruction at the beginning of the 17th century, now contains "Jyllands Herregårdsmuseum" (Jutland's Manor House Museum) with interiors from Gammel Estrup as well as from other manors in Jutland. A number of manor houses in Jutland are now open to the public for limited periods. In central Jutland this is the case for *Clausholm* (completed in 1699), the Renaissance castle *Rosenholm* and the baroque castle *Engelsholm,* which at present is a folk high school.

Among the more modern tourist attractions is the park *LEGOLAND®* which is one of the most popular in Denmark. It is a theme park, built of LEGO® bricks, representing buildings and landscapes from all parts of the world. *Givskud Zoo* is a safari park where 800 animals from all over the world can be seen in 60 hectares (150 acres) of natural surroundings.

Central Jutland is also steeped in market town culture. The historical and internationally unique *"Den Gamle By"* (The Old Town) in *Århus* consists of renovated market town buildings from the most of Denmark. This museum location even contains an historical theatre (from Helsingør on Zealand).

Århus is Jutland's largest and Denmark's second largest city. It has a cultural centre with a university, a theatre, a large concert hall and many schools. The Palace of *Marselisborg* is the summer residence of the royal family.

On the Djursland peninsular can be seen one of the most sensational landscape formations created under the ice cap. *Mols Hills,* where the highest point is 137 m. The island of Kalø is joined to Djursland by a stone causeway. *The ruin on Kalø* is the remains of a royal fortress founded in 1313.

Djursland contains the towns of *Ebeltoft* and *Grenå.* Denmark's one and only preserved wooden battleship lies in Ebeltoft, the *steam and sail frigate "Jylland"* built in the 1860s and recently restored with the recreation of the masts and yards.

Ebeltoft has crooked streets, low buildings and many beautiful half-timbered houses. The town possesses the *smallest town hall in Europe.* It dates from 1576 and now holds a folklore collection.

The *town hall in Randers* is considerably larger. In 1930 it caused an international sensation when it was put on rollers and moved 3 metres to make room for a street development.

Vejle, with some justification, is said to have the most beautiful location in Denmark - with steep, tree-covered slopes rising from a fjord, which today can be crossed by a bridge.

In the southernmost part of Central Jutland there are two localities that played an important role in Denmark's history. One is *Jelling,* which was the royal residence 1000 years ago. There are two royal burial mounds and two world famous rune stones from the period when Denmark, relatively undramatically, converted to Christianity.

The other place is *Fredericia,* founded in 1649 as a fortified town. During the summer of 1849, Fredericia was twice beseiged and bombarded by an army from Schleswig and Holstein that were formerly duchies under the Danish throne, and where the pro-German part of the population demanded independence.

The war was won by Denmark, and one of the deciding battles was fought by a militarily successful sortie from the beseiged Fredericia on 6th July 1849. The statue *"Landsoldaten"* (The Soldier) by H.W. Bissen is a memorial to this event.

A sigh of relief sounded in Denmark and everyone believed that the boundary dispute in Southern Jutland was finally resolved. However, that proved to be a terrible delusion.

In summer, the life and work of olden days is brought to life in the Old Village open-air museum on **Hjerl Hede.**

Randers Rådhus

"The Jute is stern and strong" - here in Randers symbolized by Helen Schou's "The Jutland Stallion".

The main building of **Gammel Estrup,** previously one of the country's proudest manor houses, is today the home of Jutland's Manor House Museum. The Agricultural Museum is housed in one of the barns.

Clausholm, Randers

Kalø Slotsruin

Rosenholm Castle was built in about 1560 by Rigsråd Jørgen Rosenkrantz. Here his son, the theologian Holger, nicknamed The Scholar, started a school for young men.

Ebeltoft

Fregatten "Jylland"

Århus

Marselisborg

Århus is Denmark's second largest town. A lively university town which is growing - not only physically but also in the Danes' awareness.

Århus Rådhus

The old Town open-air museum at Århus has re-erected houses showing the handicrafts and livelihoods of centuries.

Den Gamle By

Marselisborg Havn

Moesgård

Himmelbjerget

"Hjejlen", Silkeborg

Wide streams abound in the Jutland countryside. South of Silkeborg, **Gudenåen** broadens out into several lakes surrounded by wooded hills - for instance the 147 m high Himmelbjerg - giving the area its own special character.

LEGOLAND® has miniature buildings from many countries, all built of Lego bricks with astonishing accuracy and veneration. There is also a "real" Wild West town, a safety-first school and numerous other attractions. And indoors, there are Titania's Palace the Helme toy collection and the doll collection - all of international standard.

45

In the Lion's Park at Givskud, the animals roam freely about. Spectators are safely behind fences or in cars.

Jelling

Børkop

Engelsholm, Vejle

"Landsoldaten" Fredericia

Vejle, a typical East Jutland market town, is surrounded by wooden hills. The mill is the town's landmark.

South Jutland and North Schleswig

A border country with memories

The war between, on the one side Denmark and on the other side pro-German citizens of Schleswig-Holstein, lasted for 3 years 1848-1850. In the middle of the 19th Century, Schleswig and Holstein were duchies ruled by the Danish kings as dukes. The Schleswig-Holstein movement now demanded that the two territories should be under a common independent rule and that North Schleswig should become a member of the German Federation (to which Holstein already

predicted, the great powers of the time reacted negatively: England, France and Russia demanded that the constitution be revoked as it posed "a threat to the peace of Europe". The king wanted to give in to the great powers, but his government refused, and resigned in protest over the king's attitude.

A newly formed government was unable to avert a catastrophe. During the night of 1st February 1864, a greatly superior Prussian-Austrian military force crossed the border at the river Ejder.

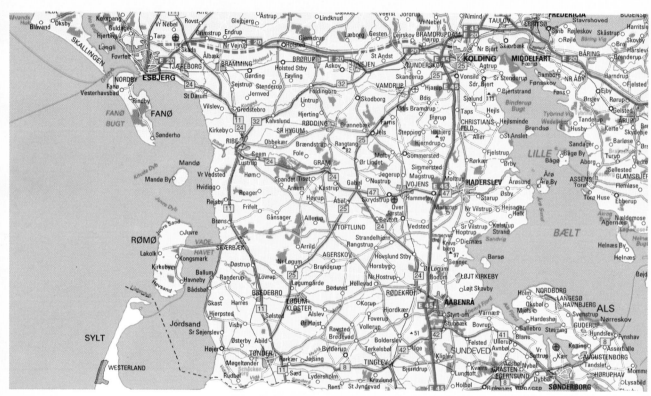

belonged). In Denmark, leading circles wanted a free constitution for the whole kingdom - including Schleswig.

Following the Danish victory in the three-years war, this point of view won a lot of support in Denmark. Furthermore, the war created antipathy between Danes and Germans which had not been the case previously.

In November 1863, the newly crowned Christian IX signed a constitution embracing both Denmark and Schleswig. He did it most unwillingly, and as he had

The attacking troops advanced through Jutland right up to Skaw. On the 30th October 1864, peace was signed in Vienna. Denmark was forced to give up Schleswig and Holstein as well as the duchy of Lauenburg. The realm was thus reduced in area by one third, and out of a population of 2½ million, about 900,000 had become Germans. Denmark was dumbfounded.

The present border between Denmark and Germany is not the border of 1864. The frequently expressed idea of a referendum was put into effect in 1920 after Germany's defeat in World War I. The referendum, which was subjected to international control, resulted in the drawing of a border which subsequently has never been contested.

Today, there is a Danish minority in Germany and a German minority in Denmark. The relations between Danes and Germans in the borderland are considered to be a model for border territories in other parts of the world. Politicians and political science researchers from all over the world come to the Danish-German borderland to study how two groups of people with different nationalities manage to live together in such harmony. As the statue of the soldier in Fredericia is a symbol of the victory in the three-year war, *Dybbøl Windmill* is a symbol of the defeat of 1864 - but also of the Danes' will to defend themselves. On 5th February 1864, the Danish main force retreated from the ancient defences, Dannevirke, to a fortified position on *Dybbøl Hills*. In spite of the enemy's superiority, the Danes held their position at Dybbøl for a surprisingly long time. The position fell on 18th April after a devastating bombardment - partly from the peninsular Broagerland, where the Prussians had a look-out post and directed the guns from one of the two spires on *Broager church*.

At the *Historical Centre, Dybbøl Hills* one can obtain insight into the Schleswig landscape and the violent events which have taken place there.

South Jutland and North Schleswig have an abundance of royal and ducal castles. In several cases, Danish royalty and Schleswigian dukes have alternated in the ownership and residency of castles in the region. Augustenborg castle on the island of Als was originally the seat of the dukes of Augustenburg. During the changing fortunes of the borderland, the Augustenburgs have also taken possession of both Sønderborg castle - now a museum containing a section that illustrates the Schleswigian wars - and Gråsten castle near Flensborg Fjord.

Gråsten castle - founded in 1709 - was taken over by Crown Prince Frederik, later Frederik IX, and Princess Ingrid. The ducal castle Shackenborg in Møgeltønder is now Prince Joachim and Princess Alexandra's home, which has resulted in a wave of tourism in the pretty North Schleswig town.

Two of the towns in the region are cathedral cities. One is *Haderslev* with its five km long lake, Haderslev

Dam, and the other, *Ribe* which is considered to be the oldest town in Denmark and was of great importance in Viking times and the Middle Ages. The oldest part of the *cathedral* was built in the 12th century.

Just south of Ribe, a six km long causeway connects North Schleswig with the island of *Rømø* which has very beautiful buildings in the Frisian style, and miles of delightful beaches.

Tønder was of great importance in the Middle Ages and the Rennaissance period as a port for the export of cattle and horses. However, since a major dam building project was initiated in the 16th century, larger ships have been unable to sail into Tønder; but the town is still connected to the North Sea by the river Vid and the lock at *Højer* on the west coast.

Esbjerg was established in 1868 as a sustitute for the export ports in the duchies which were lost in 1864. When it was founded, there were merely two farms. Today, the town is the centre for Danish export westwards and it has the biggest fishing harbour in the country with about 600 fishing vessels. Esbjerg is also notable for being the land base for the production of oil and gas in the Danish zone of the North Sea, which has had a big influence on the national economy. The population is about 80,000. In this rather new town, by Danish standards, there is great interest in the arts, not least in pictorial art. The sculpture *"People by the Sea"* is one example of art in Esbjerg.

Koldinghus in Kolding was founded as early as 1248 and has been a royal residence and venue for lavish court festivities. The castle burned down in 1808 and was later partially rebuilt. It contains an important historical exhibition and a collection of paintings.

The old lock at Højer, seen from the projecting dyke. On the water-level post beside the old lock, up to 5.33 m over mean water level has been measured.

Sønderborg

Sønderborg Castle - where shells from the 1864 attack still remain in the walls - is now a museum for the Slesvig wars and first and second world wars, besides housing cultural-historical collections from South Jutland. The castle, where Christian II was imprisoned from 1532-49, was built before 1200 as a fortress.

Gråsten Slot

Augustenborg Slot

Historiecenter Dybbøl Banke

The wars of 1848 and 1864 ended in defeat and German occupation. Until the reunion in 1920, Dybbøl Banker with the mill and battered entrenchments were a symbol of Danish patriotism in South Jutland.

Møgeltønder

Schackenborg

Profa

Profa Farver
v. Per Jacobsen

Tønder

533 m

492 m

4,36 m

4,30 m

Højer

The flood level pillar at **Højer** shows that the road is not always passable: in 1825, the water reached 5.33 m and, in 1976, 4.92 m above normal.

54

Rømø

Haderslev Domkirke

Ribe Domkirke

Koldinghus

Fanø

Esbjerg Havn

Esbjerg is, by Danish standards, a new town that has grown up around what today is the country's fifth largest harbour. A town where shipping has made its mark.

Esbjerg harbour is also the base of supply ships for the Dan Field, Denmark's first oil field from 1972, about 200 km west of Esbjerg.

"Gormfeltet", Esbjerg

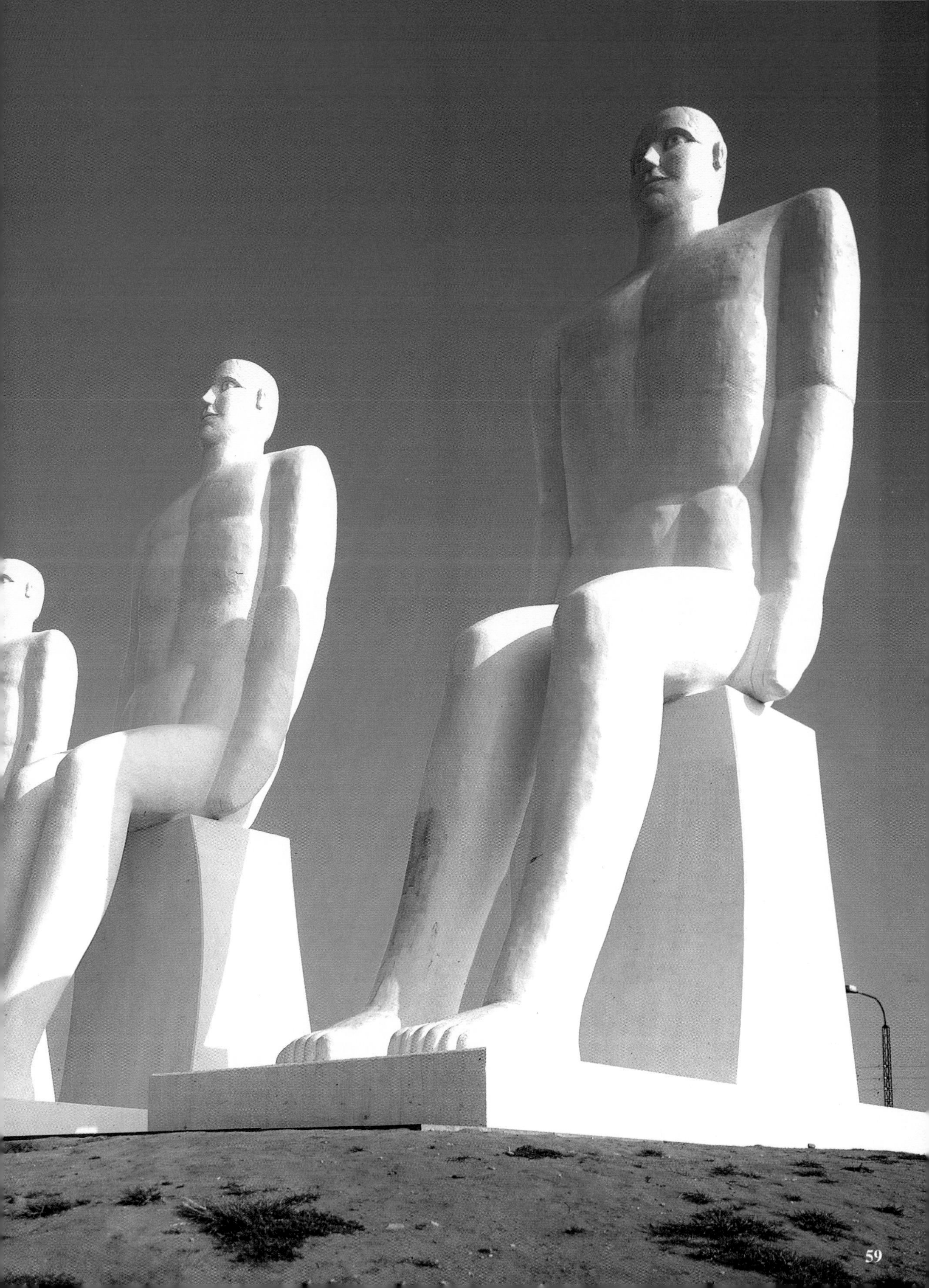

Funen

The smiling islands

By one of the two bridges connecting Jutland and Funen, one travels from the Euro-Asiatic continent - to which Jutland belongs geographically - to Denmark's second largest island, Funen, which is separated from Jutland by the Little Belt and from Zealand by the Great Belt.

An island kingdom needs bridges; though when a bridge over Little Belt was under consideration in 1930, there were many sceptics.
The Belt is over half a mile wide and nearly 100 feet deep and there is a strong current.
There were also many people who did not believe that there would be enough traffic during the last century to justify such a bridge.
Nevertheless, a railway and road bridge was built - and taken into use in 1935.

It was already clear 30 years later that the bridge was totally inadequate for the pressure of traffic. Therefore in 1970 the new Little Belt bridge was inaugurated; a six-lane motorway bridge and Denmark's first suspension bridge. Its full length over the water is 1,080 m (3,500 ft) and the middle span measures 600 m (1,968 ft).
The main cables which are suspended from two pylons, 120 m (400 ft) high, are 1,500 m (4,920 ft) long and are fastened on each side of the bridge to enormous anchor blocks.

Denmark's second largest island Funen (almost 1,800 sq.miles) is surrounded by a cluster of islands. Most of them lie south of the main island in what is called "Det sydfynske Øhav", (South Funen's Island Sea) but also the islands in Little Belt on the north coast of Funen and those in Great Belt belong geologically to the "The Funen Archipelago".
The overall area of the smaller islands is a little larger than that of the main island.

The south Funen Island Sea is a water-covered area of just under 500 sq.km (300 sq.miles) containing over 50 islands - depending on what can be considered an island, an islet or a reef. The area is bounded in the

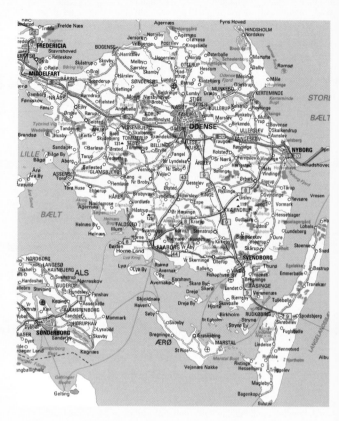

south by *Ærø* and in the east by *Langeland*. It is a paradise for yachtsmen.

Tåsinge is the third "big" island in the island sea. It is known principally for the magnificent *Valdemar's Castle*. It was originally built by Christian IV in 1639-43, but destroyed during the Swedish Wars. Its new owner, the naval hero Niels Juel, rebuilt the castle in baroque style about 1680. The castle, with its many beautiful rooms and the castle chapel are open to the public. Denmark's Museum for Yachting is housed in one wing. Nearby, in the idyllic little town of *Troense*, there is a *maritime museum* with relics from the period when the island was a base for ocean-going shipping. Funen and the other small islands are a treasure chest of historical, cultural and natural assets. Nearly all types of landscape are represented on the Funen archipelago.

The "gentleness" of the landscape of Funen is often referred to, and many observations in the course of time have assumed a possible connection between the landscape and human nature. This naturally has no basis in scientific evaluation. Nevertheless, the concept "Spring on Funen" - which has a very poetical meaning for many Danes - is the title of an oratorio by the composer Carl Nielsen who was from Funen. The landscape of Funen has also inspired a large group of important Danish artists. And it was a native of Funen who told the whole world fairytales: Hans Christian Andersen.

The storyteller's childhood surroundings are today an attraction in *Odense,* Funens biggest and Denmark's third largest town, with a population of about 168,000. *Hans Christian Andersen's* birthplace opened as a museum in 1905. The interiors hold the author's own furniture, documents, books and manuscripts. The pictures in the Hall of Memory are from Andersen's autobiography "Mit Livs Eventyr" (The Adventure of My Life). •

St. Knuds, Odense's Cathedral, is considered to be Denmark's most beautiful Gothic building. The oldest part of the present church dates from 1301.

Den fynske Landsby (a village on Funen) in Odense is an open-air museum which illustrates Funen's peasant culture. There are buildings from all parts of Funen and an open air theatre.

Funen's archipelago is rich in castles and manor houses. *Egeskov Castle* which lies between Odense and *Svendborg* is from the middle of the 16th century and is regarded as Europe's best preserved island fort.

According to tradition, a whole beechwood was felled in order to give the magnificent castle on the water a solid foundation. The style is late Gothic with a touch of Dutch Renaissance. In the large farm buildings are housed a veteran car and aeroplane museum, a collection of motorbikes, bicycles and mopeds, an agricultural and horse carriage museum - as well as a "Museum of Curiosities"!

Tranekær on Langeland, according to legend, was originally built as a fortress on - an iceberg. It is probable that parts of the present building date from the 13th century; but the building is definitely not from the ice age.

On the other hand, *Hesselagerstenen* (the Hesselager stone) is from that time and lies in all its might near the Renaissance castle Hesselagergård in east Funen. It is Denmark's biggest "erratic boulder" as it is called in ice- age terminology. It really is an enormous boulder: 12 m (36 ft) high and 46m (150 ft) in circumference. It weighs about 1,000 tons.

The town of Svendborg is very attractively situated: on one side the gentle landscape of Funen, on the other *Svendborg Strait* dividing Funen from Tåsinge. Svendborgsundbroen (Svendborg Strait Bridge) between Funen and Tåsinge is 1.220 m (4000 ft) long and Denmark's first high-pillared bridge.

In 1980, a museum was established in the yellow house where **Hans Christian Andersen** grew up. The museum contains manuscripts, letters, drawings and other items that illustrate the life of the fairy tale writer and poet.

Hollofgård

Claus Berg, the famous German wood carver, has created many works of art for Danish churches. His most well-known work is the gilded triptych, one of the largest in northern Europe, in Odense Cathedral.

Odense Rådhus

Møntergården

Odense Slot

Carl Nielsens Barndomshjem

H. C. ANDERSEN
HER LØB JEG OM MED TRÆSKOE PAA
OG GIK I FATTIGSKOLE –
HER VAR INDTIL AAR 1847 BYENS
FATTIGGAARD OG FATTIGSKOLE

South of Odense is the **Funen Village open-air museum.**

Egeskov, i.e. Oak forrest,
built in 1554, rises from the
lake on a foundation of
oak piles.
It is Northern Europe's best
preserved "water castle".
Summer concerts are
held in the banqueting hall -
and the park is a
wonderland.

Hesselager. When the Ice Age ended, the melting ice left a huge stone of about 1000 tons in the middle of Funen landscape at Hesselager.

Svendborgsund

Svendborg

Valdemar Castle is located on the island of Tåsinge, south of Funen. Built by King Christian IV in 1639-44, the castle was purchased by maritime hero Niels Juel in 1678, and is still owned by his family.

Valdemars Slot

Tranekær, Langeland

Langeland

Marstal   *Søby*

Funen is like a lovely garden, the archipelago is idyllic, but Ærø has it all. The incredibly well-kept houses, many from the 1700s, are the back-cloth of an innocent charm which characterizes the inhabitants and enchants guests. There is a nautical college at Marstal and almost everything on the island has something to do with ships.

Ærøskøbing

Zealand

Vikings, Bishops and Kings

From the middle of 1998, motorists travelling from Funen to Denmark's largest island, Zealand will cross the longest bridge in the world. They will be driving on a suspension bridge which has the longest mid-section (free hanging span) in the world and - consequently - the highest pylons in the world.

World records do not hold very long. A short time after *The Great Belt Bridge* came into use, a bridge construction in Japan was opened with even larger dimensions. The Danish bridge is impressive anyway.

The total length of the bridge is 18 km (10.9 miles), of which about 2 km (1.2 miles) have their foundations in an artificial appendage to the little island of Sprogø in the Great Belt. The main length of the construction is divided between a low bridge connecting Funen with Sprogø and a high bridge - the suspension bridge between Sprogø and Zealand. The middle section (free hanging span) of the high bridge is 1,624 m (about 1 mile) long and the bridge pylons have the formidable height of 254 m (770 ft).

Denmark's biggest island, Zealand (7,015 sq.km - 2,709 sq.miles) has an attractive landscape and many fascinating testimonies from pre-history and the historical past.

Christianity was introduced into Viking Denmark in the 9th and 10th centuries, when "historical time" originated, e.g. the period from which relics and reports can be interpreted and construed with great accuracy.

One of the oldest and most significant relics from the Viking Age is *Trelleborg,* near Slagelse. It is a naval-military "barracks", and it is supposed that warriors came sailing up the nearby River Tude and pulled their magnificent ships onto the dry land.

Næstved, which is south Zealand's biggest town is situated on its longest river, *Susåen,* and contrary to the fire-ravaged Copenhagen, has managed to conserve its medieval architecture, first and foremost the town hall.

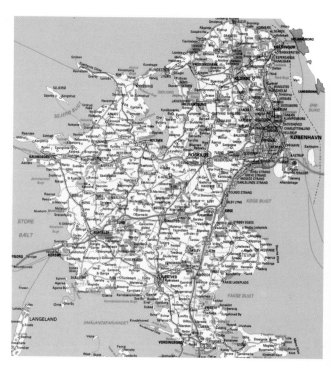

Gavnø castle just south of Næstved is world famous for its flower gardens. The castle is also internationally renowned as a monument to the Age of Enlightenment in 18th century Europe. On his death in 1785, the founder left the biggest collection of paintings in Scandinavia; mostly portraits, but also landscapes and conversation pieces by Old Masters such as Rubens, Jordaens, Hals, Snyders and Ruisdal. He had also succeeded in collecting a great many books for Gavnø's library - 138,000 volumes.

Large areas of North Zealand have belonged to the crown for centuries, and the territory which is rich in lakes and forests, holds extensive hunting grounds. The little castle and hunting lodge, *Eremitagen* just north of Copenhagen testifies to this.

The Renaissance castle *Kronborg* at the entrance to *Øresund* (The Sound) at *Helsingør* was built in the reign of Frederik II (1559-1588). The building was greatly admired in contemporary Europe. William Shakespeare made the castle the setting for his drama "Hamlet, Prince of Denmark" (1599). The castle of *Frederiksborg* in Hillerød is Christian IV's greatest showpiece. Today it contains the National History Museum.

Fredensborg, which lies on Lake Esrom, is from the 1720's and was erected in the reign of Frederik IV in commemoration of peace in the (supposed) last war between Denmark and Sweden. The castle, which is still a royal residence in the Spring and Autumn, was famous in Europe at the end of the 19th century as the meeting place of the royal families.

Rungstedlund in Rungsted is open to the public in memory of the authoress, Karen Blixen (1885-1962). *Louisiana* in Humlebæk is a very popular centre for modern art.
South of Copenhagen, a centre for modern art was opened in 1995 in Ishøj, on the Bay of Køge. It is called *Arken* (The Ark) and is housed in a much admired building, which has the appearance of a ship.

The Ark stands in the middle of an extensive recreational area - Køge Strandpark - with 7 km of bathing beaches backed by beautiful natural surroundings. This area was planned as a supplement to the traditional bathing beach for Copenhageners, Bellevue, just north of the city. Many people still go there to enjoy the seaside, but it is very crowded.

There is a whole little fleet of Viking ships in *Roskilde.* The ships were recovered from the bottom of the fjord (the latest in 1996). It is now possible to sail on the fjord in exact replicas.

The bishopric Roskilde contains the magnificent cathedral *Roskilde Domkirke,* the oldest part of which is from the 13th century. Since the 15th century the cathedral has been the burial place of the Danish monarchs. The diocese of Roskilde founded Denmark's present capital, *Copenhagen,* which in the beginning was a sort of offshoot of Roskilde.

The baroque castle *Ledreborg* near Roskilde is a testimony of absolute monarchy in Denmark. It was built for one of the highest ranking despotic officials in the middle of the 18th century. By then, though, Copenhagen had been the seat of royal power for a long time.

Storebæltsbroen

Trelleborg, Slagelse

Kalundborg

Lerchenborg

Every spring thousands of tulips bloom in **Gavnø's park.**

Gavnø

Susåen, Næstved

Roskilde Cathedral's history began in the Viking era when Harald Bluetooth - who christianized the Danes - built a church here in 980. The present was begun in 1170 and is the burial place of the Danish kings.

Ledreborg

The **Roskilde Viking Ship Museum** exhibits, builds and researches.

Roskilde Kloster

Rungstedlund

Eremitagen, Klampenborg

Arken, Ishøj

Louisiana, Humlebæk

Louisiana, the museum at Humlebæk, exhibits Danish and international art from after 1950. Changing exhibitions from the world's finest collections are also shown here.

Fredensborg, i.e. Castle of Peace, built in 1722, is the Queen's spring and autumn residence.

Hillerød

The main part of **Frederiksborg Castle** was built in 1600-25 and is a major architectural work of the Danish Renaissance. Today, it houses an historical museum.

Helsingør

Holger Danske

Frederik II built **Kronborg,** i.e. the Castle of the Crown, on the site of the old Krogen castle. It was finished in 1585 to become one of Northern Europe's most beautiful castles.
It was here that The Sound Dues were charged.

The image shows a historical bird's-eye view illustration of Copenhagen with labels including: Arsenal, Orlogshavn, Sextus, Lynet, Langelinie, Citadel, Østerbro, and Sortedams-Sö.

Copenhagen

The foundation of the first fortress in Copenhagen occurred in 1167 - on the same spot where one today sees *Christiansborg* with the parliament (Folketinget), royal reception rooms and the highest court in the land, Højesteret. Copenhagen is a city from the middle ages and the street patterns from the earliest time are preserved in the inner city so that the atmosphere is "medieval". However, there are very few remains of medieval buildings due to three extensive and devastating fires in the 18th and 19th centuries. The oldest fully conserved building is from the Renaissance period, constructed in the reign of Christian IV (1588-1648) - and built with the active participation of this colourful Renaissance king. He involved himself first and foremost in the building of the fairytale palace *Rosenborg* and Trinitatis, the complex with the University church, astronomical centre and the world famous observatory and look-out tower *Rundetårn*.

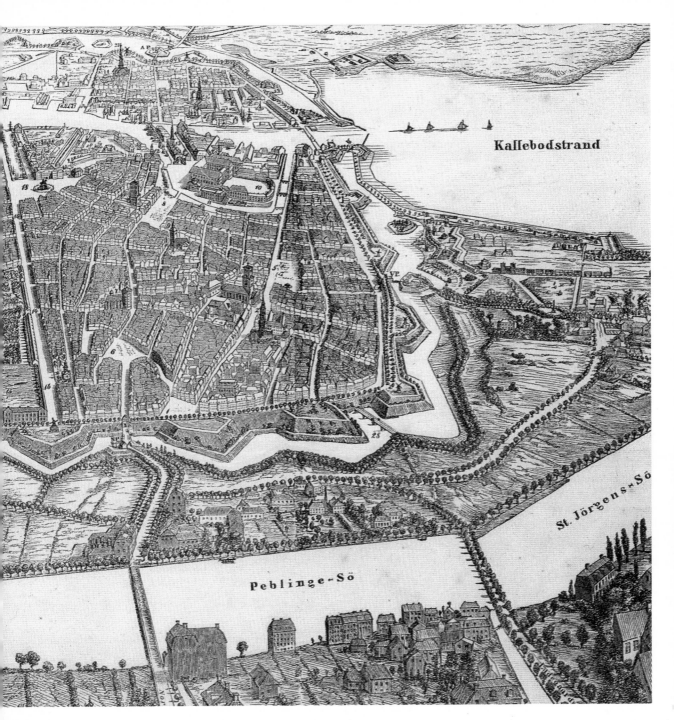

Another international star in Copenhagen is *The Little Mermaid,* inspired by Hans Christian Andersen's story. Measured by the millions of admirers of this small, unpretentious sculpture, it is just as famous as the Statue of Liberty in New York's harbour - and definitely prettier.

A third world celebrity is *Tivoli,* opened in 1843 and today a uniquely preserved tradition for the expression of music, entertainment and amusements, all at very high standards, especially classical music.

Classicism from the 19th century is dominant in the cityscape of Copenhagen. The cathedral Vor Frue Kirke (The Church of Our Lady) is a prominent example. The *Glyptothek* contains a distinguished collection of sculptures based on classicism, but also encompassing antique and modern art.

The royal residence of *Amalienborg,* where the *Royal Lifeguards* keep watch, was built in the middle of the 18th century.

Rådhuspladsen

"Den lille Havfrue"

Gefion Springvandet

Kastellet

Langelinie

The **Royal Life Guards** was founded in 1658. The bearskin busby and the cartridge pouch belong among the best known details in the history of military uniforms. The Life Guards are an infantry regiment and most of the soldiers have volunteered to do their military service there. The regiment's most important right and duty is to protect the royal family.

The **Changing of the Guard** – a big attractions for both the people of Copenhagen and tourists – takes place on Amalienborg Palace every day at 12 p.m. and the guards march from and to their barracks at Rosenborg Castle. The march through the city lasts about an hour by different routes. The Guard's band accompanies only when the Queen is in residence at Amalienborg.

The houses in **Nyhavn** (New Harbour) look as did when H.C. Andersen lived there. Once upon a time the old salts hung out here, and one can still get a tattoo. Today, most of the sailors come from the yachts that lie along the quay. There are amusing shops and a varied selection of restaurants and cafes; some are good eating places, others pay more attention to the music.

Nyhavn

Vor Frelser Kirke

Christianshavn

Christiansborg

Vesterbro

"Diamanten"

Glyptoteket

Tivoli, København

Tivoli, København

Vesterport

Hovedbanegården

Tycho Brahe Planetarium & SAS Royal Hotel

Helligåndskirken

The longest pedestrian street in Europe lies in Copenhagen. It stretches from Rådhuspladsen (City Hall Square) over Gammel Torv, (Old Market Square) Amagertorv and Bremerholm to Kongens Nytorv (Kings New Market Square). We call it **"Strøget"** and here you can find everything from old-fashioned clock-makers to large, modern department stores.

Rundetaarn

Christian IV's building projects where influenced by Dutch Renaissance style – and by Christian IV. **Rosenborg** was his "summerhouse". Today it houses the **Danish Kings Chronological Collection** – a world famous and unique collection which contains the Danish crown jewels. The crown shown here is one of them.

Statens Museum for Kunst

The **"Øresundsbron"** connects Denmark to Sweden and was opened on 1st July 2000. It consists of an immersed tunnel, an artificial island and a bridge. The bridge itself has a total length of 7.845 metes.

Grundtvigs Kirke

Lolland, Falster and Møn

Medieval treasures and fairytale castles

The two largest islands lying just south of Zealand in the Baltic are nearly always named in conjunction; Lolland-Falster. They also lie close together and are connected by two short bridges. Until 1937 the only access to the rest of the country was by ship.

Storstrøm's Bridge between Zealand (Masnedø) and Falster, which was the most ambitious bridge building project of the 1930's, was inaugurated in 1937.

in Denmark to date. The section between Falster and Farø is connected by a suspension bridge of a different type than the Little Belt and Great Belt bridges. The distance between Falster and Farø is about 1.7 km (1 mile), over Farø almost 1 km (0.6 mile) and between Farø and Zealand almost 1.6 km (1 mile).

Just as in the 1930's, bridge building in the 1990's makes many people feel wistful; there has always been a certain romance about sailing on ferries. However, there will always be a need for ferries in Denmark.

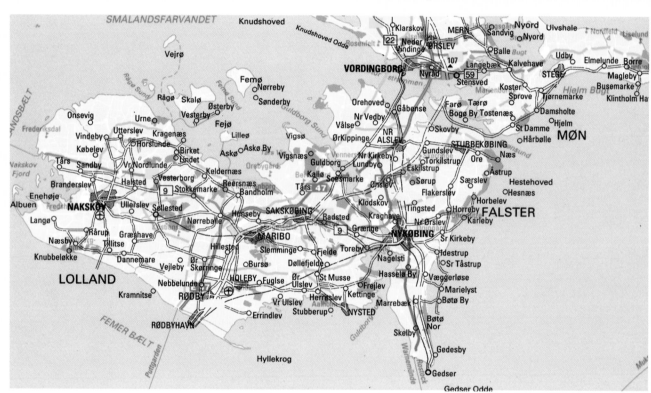

The background for bridge building during this period was mass unemployment in Denmark and other European countries. It takes many hands for a considerable period of time to build a large bridge.

Storstrøm's Bridge is the same type as Little Belt Bridge from 1935 - the load-bearing construction of steel, the foundations and roadway of cement - but is much longer; nearly 3.2 km (2 miles).

The modern Farø bridges, Zealand-Farø-Falster, are considered to be the most elegant bridge constructions

Among the many islands there will always be places where one will need (and surely be glad) to avoid the stress and strain of modern travel.

Lolland's area is 1,234 sq.km. (480 sq.miles), Falster's 514 sq.km (198 sq.m) and Møn's 216 sq.km (84 sq.m). Larger towns on the islands are Nykøbing Falster, Nakskov and Maribo on Lolland and Stege on Møn.
(In Denmark there are 3 towns called Nykøbing. It is therefore an obvious practicality to appendage the county name to the town in all three cases).

There is a medieval feeling to the buildings in these three towns. *Middelaldercentret* (Medieval Centre) at Nykøbing Falster is from modern times; it is an open-air museum which gives an impression of life and conditions in the Middle Ages.

The smallest genuine town milieu in Denmark is found in *Nysted* on Lolland. The abbey around which the town grew up has long since vanished, but the well-preserved medieval church is stil there. A causeway connects Nysted to *Aalholm Castle,* which in appearance looks like a massive medieval fortress. In modern times, a large and impressive collection of veteran cars belonging to the castle's owner is internationally famous. Aalholm's Veteran Car Museum is open to the public for most of the year.

The eastern end of *Møn* consists of glacial deposits that rest on chalk. In the Baltic Sea, the chalk breaks the surface and forms the 7-8 km (5 mile) long *Møns Klint,* that rises sheer from the sea, reaching a height of 128 m (420 ft).

Liselund on Møn was intended to be a fairytale castle - and so it is. It was devised and financed by a very rich court official in the 1790's - as a present for a young woman who was a great beauty of her time, with whom he was very much in love. Her name was Lisa Iselin.

Lisa Iselin had a favourite seat on a bench near Møns Klint. One day, to her astonishment, she noticed a statue by the bench which had not been there before.

The estate *Knuthenborg* on Lolland has some magnificent examples of buildings in English rural style, from the 1860's.
A deerpark was established, which by the standards of those days was progressive, as amongst other animals it contained Canadian red deer, wapitis, muflons and guanacos.
Today it has been taken a step further: the park, which is open to the public every day, is also a playground for Asian and African species of animals, among which are *tigers* and *giraffes,* which thrive perfectly well on Lolland.

It pictured the Graces (goddesses of beauty), but there were only two and not three as in the classical model. On examination she found an inscription that had been written by Liselund's patron. "They are waiting for their sister." She became his wife.

Farøbroen

Lalandia is mostly known for its waterpark with tropical temperatures (water min. 28° C – air min. 30°C). It also offers entertainment, sports, good food and some very family-friendly holiday homes.

Lalandia

Maribo rådhus

Maribo is beautifully situated at Søndersø, in central Lolland. The picturesque town hall is from the middle of the last century but the town has a municipal charter from 1416.

Aalholm Manor is not only a splendid 800-year-old building, but it also houses an automobile museum of unique international standard.

Aalholm Slot, Nysted

Middelaldercentret, Nykøbing Falster

In about 1870, Count E.C. Knuth transformed the fields and woods of **Knuthenborg** into a **park** of enormous dimensions surrounded by a 7 km long stone wall. He planted rare trees and plants, many from the farthest corners of the earth. Now the huge trees, enormous rhododendrons and other botanical rarities make a unique frame for Northern Europe's largest safari park.

Møn

Dr. Alexandrines Bro

Fanefjord Kirke

Liselund Slot

Liselund ny Slot

Bornholm

Drama in the landscape - and in history

Just as in northernmost Denmark one speaks of "The light over Skaw", so do those in the most easterly region speak of "The light over Bornholm".

Sunlight is reflected in wide expanses of sea surface - and here it is to the horizon in every direction. Like Skaw, Bornholm has attracted painters and other types of artists. The best known are Oluf Høst and Olaf Rude.

By Danish geographical standards, Bornholm lies far to the east of the rest of the kingdom, in the Baltic, southeast of the now Swedish territory, Skåne. The island is connected by various ferry routes as well as to Copenhagen by a plane service - that flies over Sweden. During the summer, when tourists from all over the world flock to Bornholm, there is also a plane service between Hamburg in North Germany and Rønne on Bornholm.

The area of Bornholm is 588 sq.km (227 sq.miles) and the stable population about 50,000. Most of the island has entirely different forms of landscape from the rest of Denmark. The island is the southern tip of bedrock which is common to the whole of the Scandinavian peninsular.

The surface of the rest of Denmark consists of a layer of deposits from the ice ages - up to 200 m (650 ft) thick - on top of deposits from even earlier periods of Earth's history. Underneath these deposits is found the bedrock.

On Bornholm, the bedrock is visible. The rock rears up to 162 m (530 ft) above sea level (at Rytterknægten). The northenmost two-thirds of the island consists of granite with a very thin layer of deposits, or none at all. At the coast, there are cliffs with vertical walls and deep clefts. One can

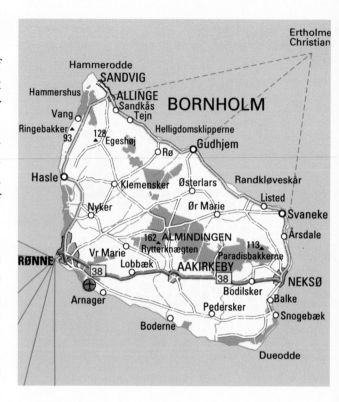

see how the granite has been ground down by the ice cap and weathered by wind and water. Melt water has created valleys (for example *Døndalen*) and Echo Valley which run for miles through the landscape.

In the middle of the island, the glacial deposits are very thin. Here were formerly heaths and moors which today are planted with trees. In the southern part, the deposits are as thick as in most of the rest of Denmark; here the land is fertile and cultivated. Measured by employment and turnover, agriculture is Bornholm's main industry, but fishing from the coastal towns is also of great importance to the economic life of the island.

A third industry on Bornholm is mining (granite, china clay for porcelain and stoneware, fireclay and sandstone).

The history of the island is as dramatic as its landscape. When Denmark lost territories in the modern southern part of Sweden after a military defeat in 1658, Bornholm also became Swedish: but the Bornholmers were not prepared to put up with that. The same year, they themselves drove the Swedes off the island, and two years later gave Bornholm back to the Danish crown - for certain priviliges for the island and military protection from the threat from Sweden.

The fortress *Hammershus* on the Bornholm's northern point which today is a picturesque ruin, was raised in the 13th century by the archbishopric of Lund in Skåne (which was then Danish) as a defence against the power of the monarchy. After the reformation in Denmark in 1536, the fortress was taken over by the crown. For many years it was used as a state prison for very high ranking prisoners.

Bornholm's medieval *round churches* with their massive walls and tiny windows were intended as fortifications in the event of attack from north, south, east or west.

The German capitulation in North Europe in May 1945 developed into a tragedy for Bornholm. In their agreements for drawing new borders at the cessation of hostilities, the victorious powers - the Western Powers and the Soviet Union - had simply forgotten about the Danish island in the Baltic that lay far to the east of the demarcation line - the later "iron curtain" which ran through the continent of Europe.

The island's German commander would surrender neither to the Soviet forces nor to the Danish underground movement on Bornholm, even though the people of Bornholm begged him to do so. The Soviet Union decided to force a capitulation by military means and conducted three air raids against the two biggest towns, *Rønne* and Neksø.

Before the third and heaviest attack by bombs and cannons, the Soviet high command had given the civil Danish authorities time to evacuate the whole population from the two towns. One citizen in Rønne - an old lady - refused point blank to be moved. She had talked to God about the affair and had decided to "stay in her nest" as she put it.

The attack lasted for 55 minutes. The old lady survived. In spite of a painful loss of human life and valuable properties, Bornholm survived also.

Rønne Havn

Svaneke Havn

Hasle

Gudhjem

Allinge

Gudhjem

Østerlars Kirke

Ruts Kirke

123

Hammerknuden

Hammershus / Vang

Døndalen

NaturBornholm

Nylars Kirke

Arnager

As a contrast to the gentle rolling landscape in the rest of the country, **Bornholm in the Baltic** is rugged, rocky coasts broken by smiling sandy beaches.

Hammershus Fortress and the four round churches, built as a mixture of church and fortress with metre-thick granite walls and embrasures, bear witness of Bornholm's violent past.

Further information

In addition, Grønlund's Forlag has produced a book "Wonderful Copenhagen", which in 80 pages and with many beautiful photos describes Copenhagen, its inhabitants, the Royal Family, places of interest and the history behind them. (The book has been issued in English, German, Italian, Spanish and Japanese, paperback and at about DKK 100. In the same series, there are also the books "Wonderful Roskilde" (32 pages, paperback at about DKK 50) and Wonderful Denmark (80 pages, hardcover at about DKK 100).

Grønlund's Forlag has also issued a book about Hans Christian Andersen's character The Little Mermaid. "The Little Mermaid - Her Story - the Writer and the Fairy Tale" (64 pages, English text. Price about DKK 50).

© KINA ITALIA S.p.A. - GRØNLUND'S FORLAG

Text: Per Eilstrup and Grønlund's Forlag
Translated by: Vivian Hovmand

Maps: Folia/Legindkort A/S

Photos: Jørgen Grønlund, Dino Sassi, Rigmor Mydtskov, Christian Erichsen, Nikolaj Meding, Steen Evald, Peter Grønlund, Lone Kjæhr, Mogens Dam, Mikkel Grønlund, Werner Karrasch, Klaus Møller, Peter Marling/Biofoto, Aage Pedersen, Michael Langeland Jensen, Vivian Nielsen, Jens Sigsgaard, Erik Thomsen/Biofoto, Svend Tougaard/Biofoto, Ole M. Johnsen, Arne V. Petersen, Solhaug Foto, Ole Woldbye, Jens Frederiksen, Jørn Freddie, Karsten Schnack/Biofoto, John Nielsen/Biofoto, Leif Schack-Nielsen/Biofoto, Svend Berning/Biofoto, Helge V. Qvistorff, Gert S. Larsen & Aerodan Luftfoto.

ISBN: 87-91087-43-0

KINA ITALIA S.p.A.
Piazza Aspromonte 15 - I - 20131 Milan
e-mail: kina@kinaitalia.it

GRØNLUND'S FORLAG
Kirkevejen 266 - DK - 4930 Maribo
e-mail: gronlunds@gronlunds.dk